Who Likes the Rain?

Written by
Etta Kaner

Illustrated by
Marie Lafrance

Kids Can Press

Who likes the rain?